SMART BRAIN RIGHT BRAIN

Learn to Draw

Om KIDZ

An imprint of Om Books International

First Published in 2021 by

Om Kidz | Om Books International

Corporate & Editorial Office
A-12, Sector 64, Noida 201 301
Uttar Pradesh, India
Phone: +91 120 477 4100
Email: editorial@ombooks.com
Website: www.ombooksinternational.com

Sales Office
107, Ansari Road, Darya Ganj
New Delhi 110 002, India
Phone: +91 11 4000 9000
Email: sales@ombooks.com

Author: Swayam Ganguly
Editor: Nandita Bhardwaj
Art & Design: Anshuman Pandey, Gaurav Bhandari, Harish Arya

ISBN: 978-93-5276-851-6

Printed in India

10 9 8 7 6 5 4 3 2 1

CONTENTS

POCKET FACT

Human beings learnt to draw before they learnt to write.

1. Introduction

I drew a lovely house, and wanted to draw more,
So I drew a few blue windows and a black door.
I also drew a brown gate that swung open
To welcome my guests in the green garden,
Where lovely red roses smiled in welcome.
Wouldn't a house like that be awesome?

Who doesn't want to learn to draw? When you learn to draw, you not only learn something new but you also have a lot of fun. Get the little artist in you ready.

2. Drawing Tools

Before you begin drawing, you would need art supplies. That means you need:

Paper

You will have to buy loose sheets of paper or a sketchbook.

Pencils

When you begin your first drawing lesson, use pencils. There are different types of pencils; some will make dark markings, and some will make light markings.

There are colour pencils also that you can use to colour your drawing.

Hold your pencil the correct way: Make sure you hold your pencil as shown in the picture. This is the right pencil grip when you draw.

Erasers

Erasers are made of rubber and they help to get rid of any marks made by mistake.

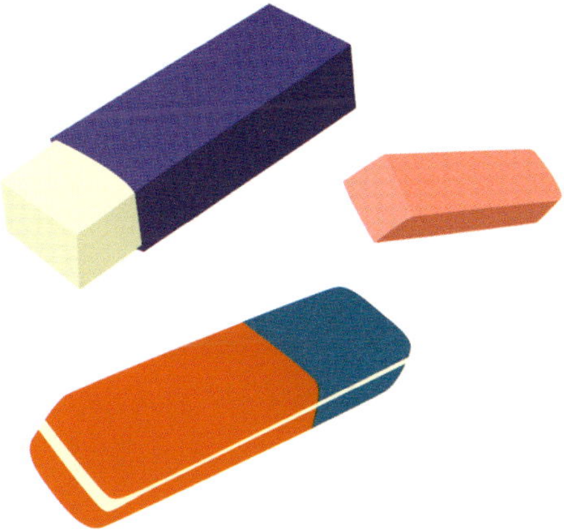

Crayons and Watercolours

Crayons and watercolours are used for colouring. Start your art lesson by using crayons, and once you are better at colouring, you can use watercolours.

Brushes

There are many types of brushes, from thin brushes to thick brushes, which you can use to colour.

3. Lines

Lines are the different movements that a pencil makes. Some are straight lines and some are curved. Learning these will help you draw better.

Horizontal

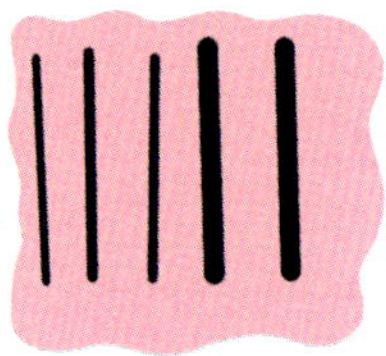
Vertical

Diagonal

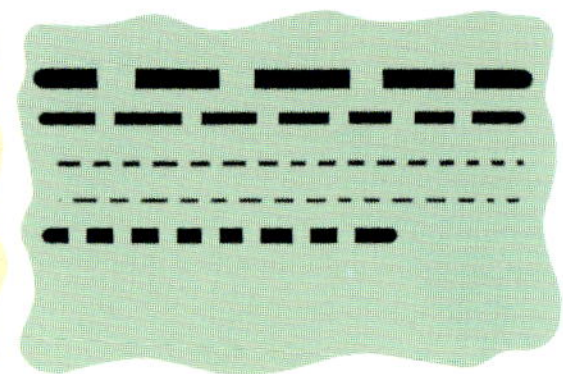
Broken

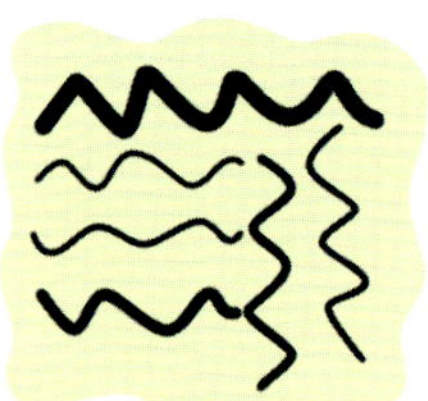
Zigzag

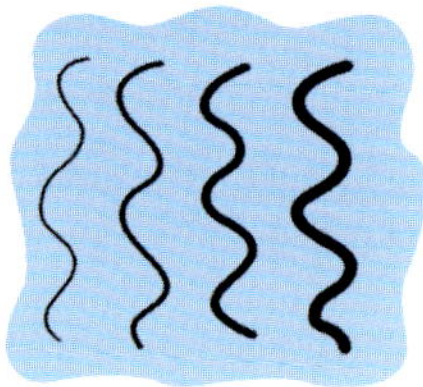
Wavy

Curved

Spiral

Hold the pencil and:

1. Move your pencil up and down and make a vertical line. You can call it the standing line.

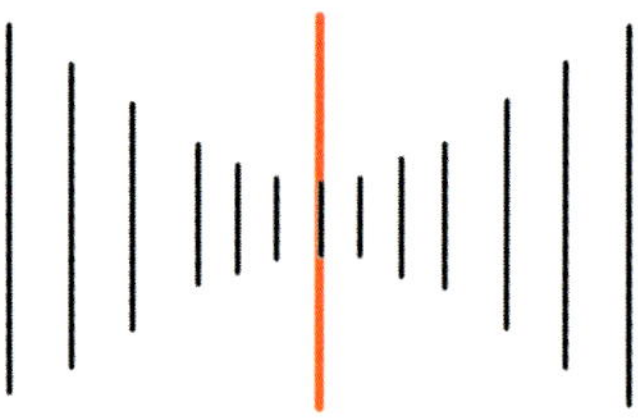

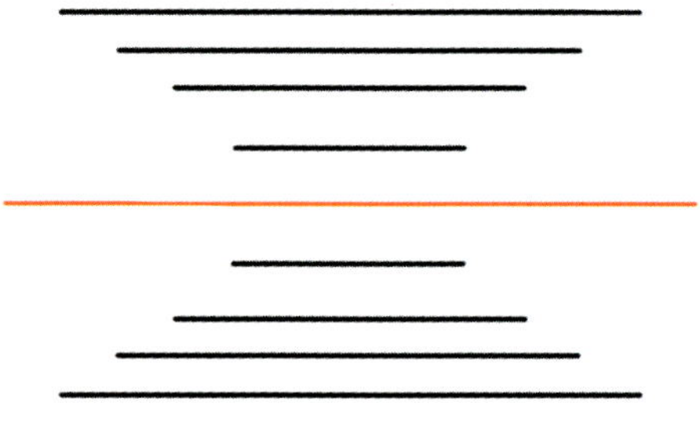

2. Move your pencil back and forth on the paper and make a horizontal line. You can also call it the sleeping line.

3. Place your pencil tip in the centre and move it towards the right side, and then towards the left on the paper. These are slanting lines.

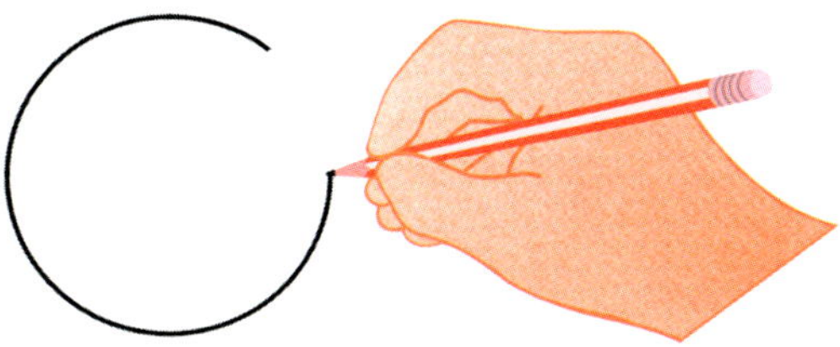

4. Place the tip of your pencil on the paper and move it in a circular motion. The round movement of the pencil means you are drawing a circle.

5. You can move your pencil in a sharp zigzag motion or a more rounded zigzag like waves.

6. Place the tip of your pencil on the paper and start making a circle. Keep increasing the size of the circle. You are making a spiral.

7. Jab the pencil tip on to the paper and make a dotted line.

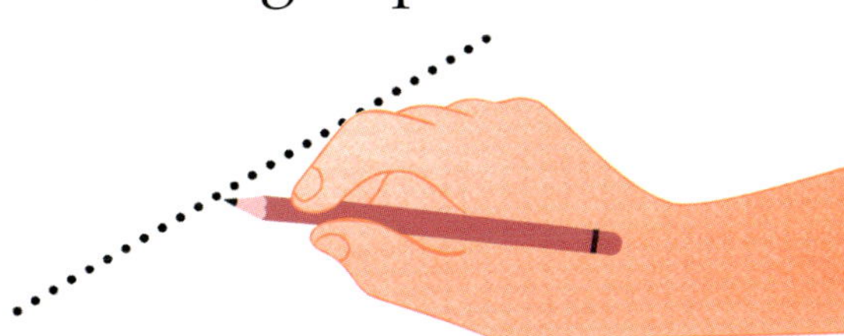

4. Shapes

Drawing with Lines

Let us take a look at the different types of shapes you can draw using straight lines.

Square

A square is four-sided where all the four sides are equal in length. Examples of a square shape are a window or a table.

Triangle

A triangle is a three-sided shape with three edges. The best examples of a triangle are the pyramids.

Rectangle

A rectangle is a shape that has four sides, where only the opposite sides are equal and parallel to each other. All rectangles have a length and a breadth. Some examples of a rectangle are a brick, a television set, and a box.

Pentagon

A pentagon is a five-sided shape. For example, the leather patch on your football.

Hexagon

A hexagon is a six-sided shape. A section of a beehive or your pencil are examples of a hexagon shape.

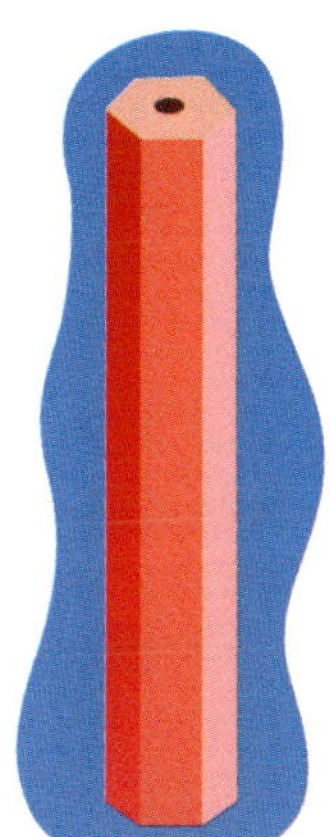

Now let us join different lines to make shapes.

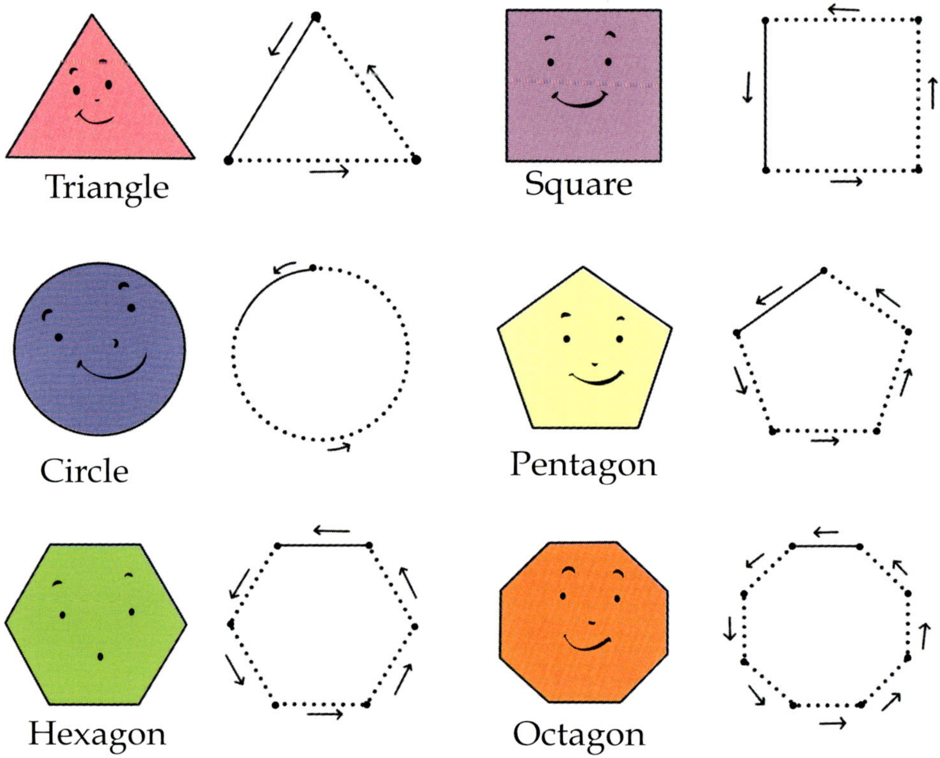

Drawing with Curves

Circle

A circle is where all the points are at an equal distance from the centre. Some examples of a circle are the wheels and the balls.

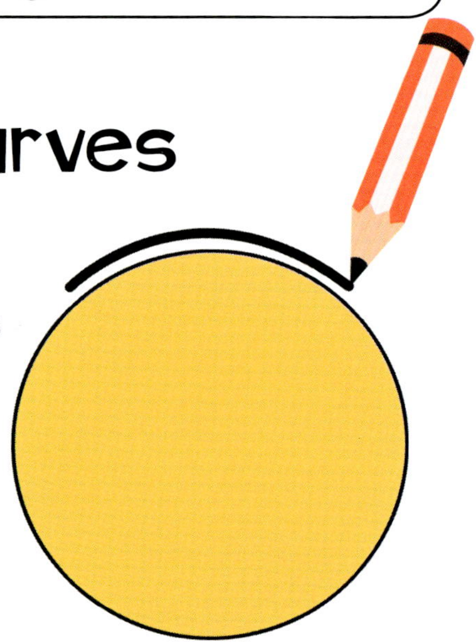

You can also draw a big C or half a circle or a big N and a big opposite C or N. You can draw a long curve that looks like a big snake and one that looks like a big U.

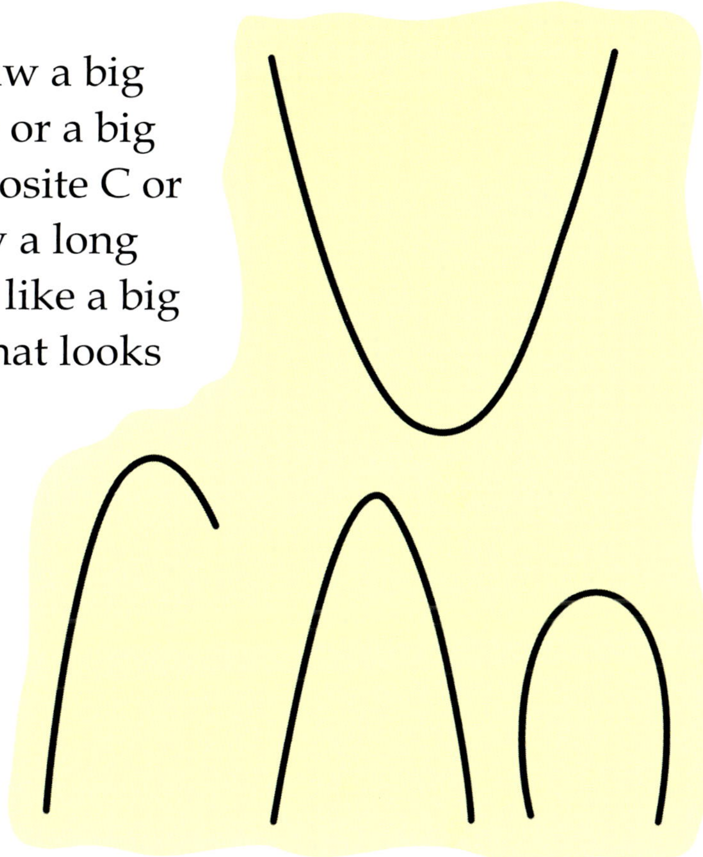

A curved line is a line that turns or bends. Curved lines often look like waves.

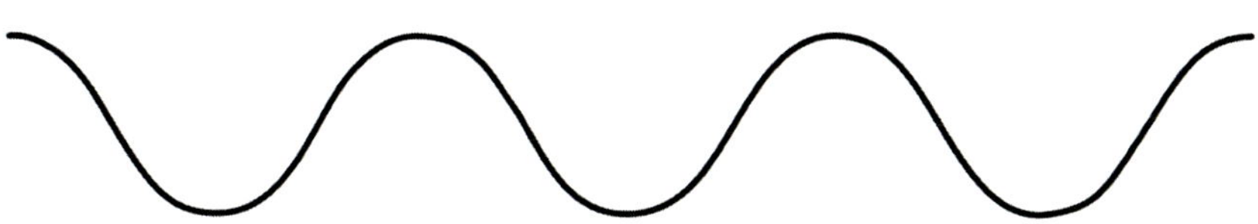

DID YOU KNOW?

The first pencils were painted yellow. This was because the colour yellow means respect and royalty.

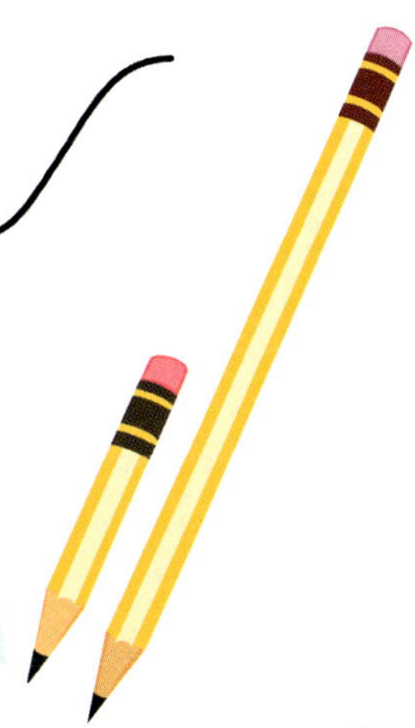

Activity

1. Let's combine lines and curves to make a double scoop ice-cream cone in seven easy steps:

Step 1: Draw two slanted lines to make a V or a triangle.

Step 2: Draw small curves to make half of a single scoop.

Step 3: Draw small curves to make the double scoop.

Step 4: Let's make a small circle which looks like a small cherry on top.

Step 5: Draw slanting lines on the V to start shading the cone.

Step 6: Draw opposite slanting lines now and your cone is ready.

Step 7: Now colour your ice-cream cone to make it look the best double scoop ice-cream.

2. Now, try your hand at making a house using lines and curves. Complete the picture.

POCKET FACT

By using these lines you can draw almost anything.

3. Let's practise:

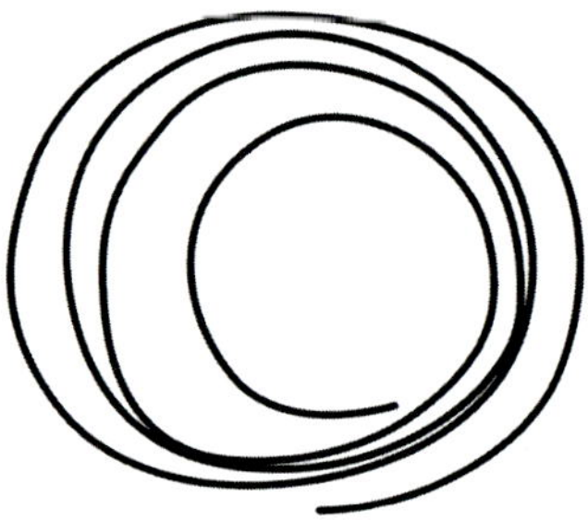

Round and Round

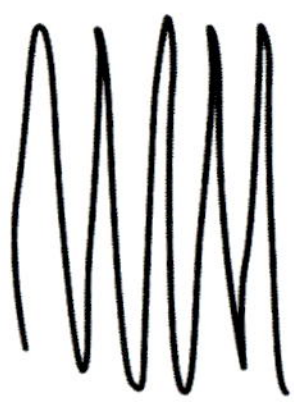

Up and Down

Back and Forth

Zigzag

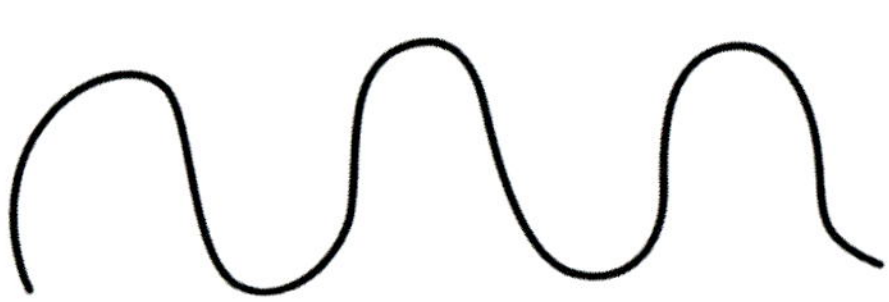

Wiggle Wiggle

Dot Dot

5. Solid Shapes

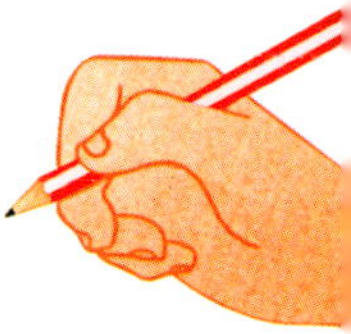

Solid shapes are not flat but occupy space. You can also call them 3D. They have corners, edges and faces. That is, they have length, width and depth. When you add depth to a square it becomes a cube, or a circle becomes a sphere and a triangle becomes a cone.

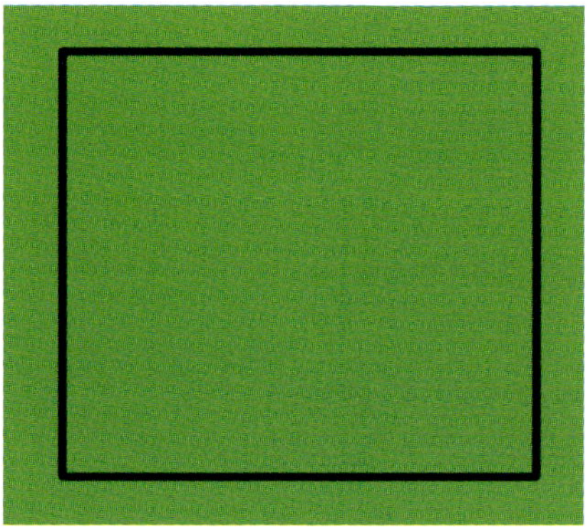

Let us draw a cube:

Step 1: Draw a square.

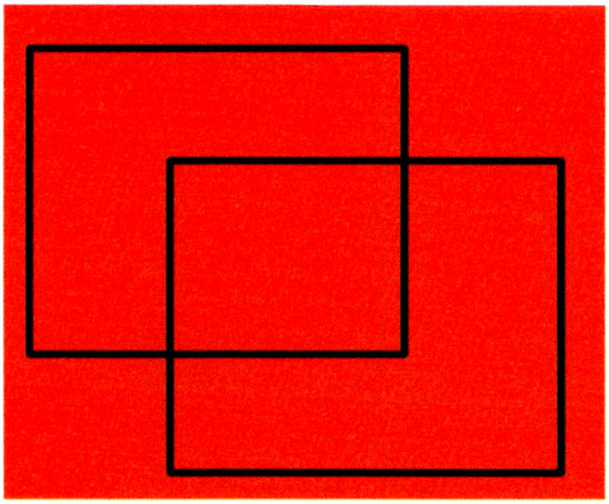

Step 2: Draw a second square above and to the left of the first square.

Step 3: Connect the bottom left corner of the first square to the bottom left corner of the second square. Do this for every corner.

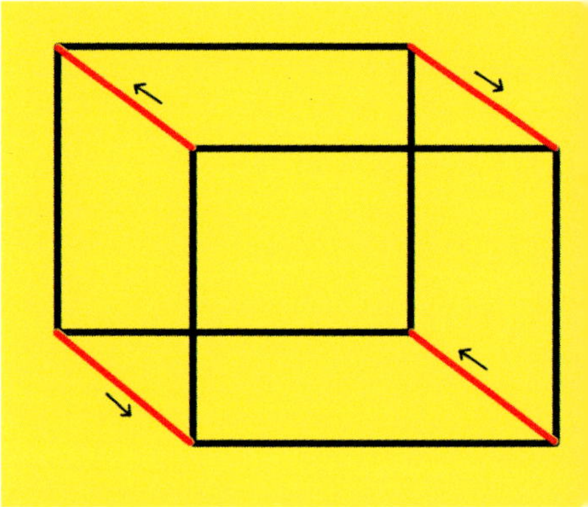

Step 4: Erase the lines that you don't need. There! You now have a cube.

Let us draw an open box out of a cube:

Step 1: Draw the lid of an open box as shown.

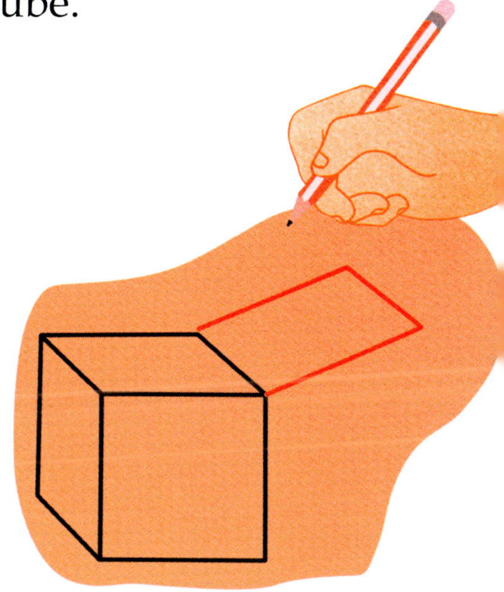

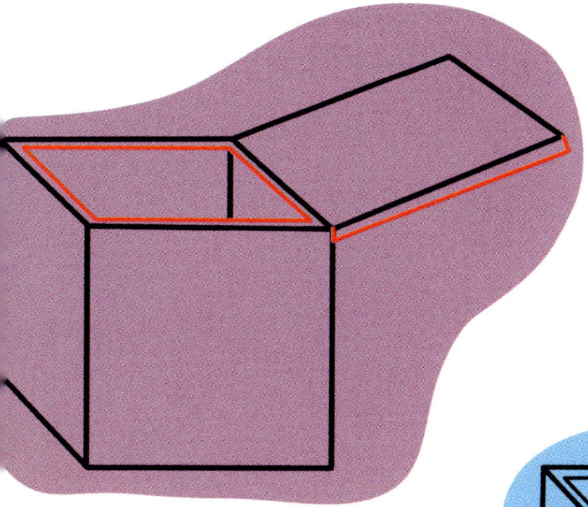

Step 2: Draw the lines inside the box also so that it looks like a box with a lid.

Step 3: Final drawing of the box with an open lid.

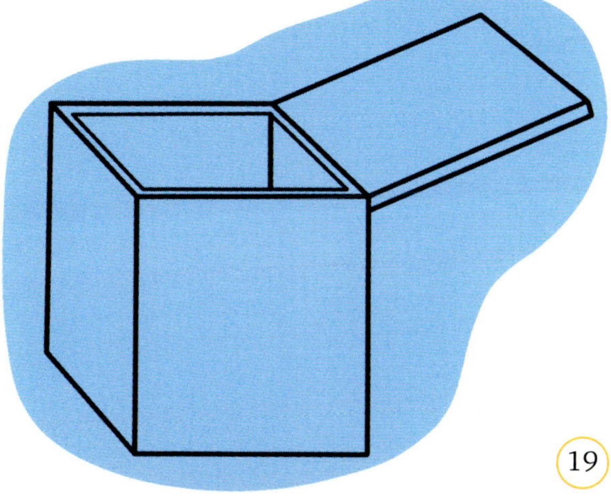

Let's learn how to turn a triangle into a cone.

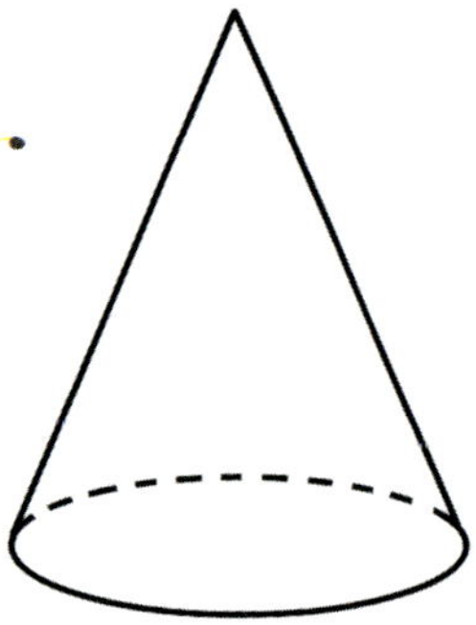

Let us learn to draw a simple house out of a cube:

Step 1: Begin making a roof on the cube by adding two triangles.

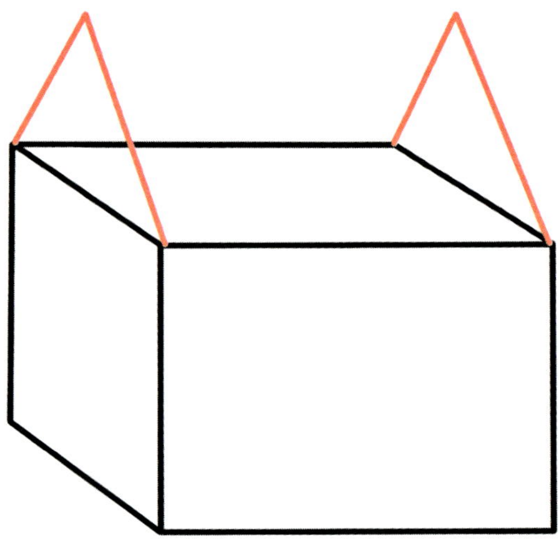

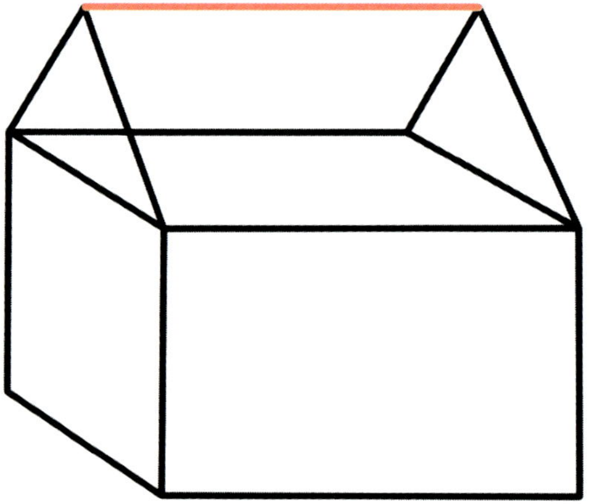

Step 2: Finish the roof by joining the triangles.

Step 3: Complete the house by making a chimney, door and windows. Now, you can also add other things in your drawing like smoke coming out of the chimney, birds flying in the sky and a small garden beside your house.

6. Drawing with Letters and Numbers

Drawing with Letters

You can use letters to make drawing even more fun. Using letters in your drawing helps you learn them as you draw.

We all know that B stands for Bird. But do you know that you can draw a bird out of the letter B? Here's how to do it.

B = Bird

In the same way, C is for Cat and J is for Jug. Let's draw a cat and a jug with the letters C and J respectively.

C = Cat

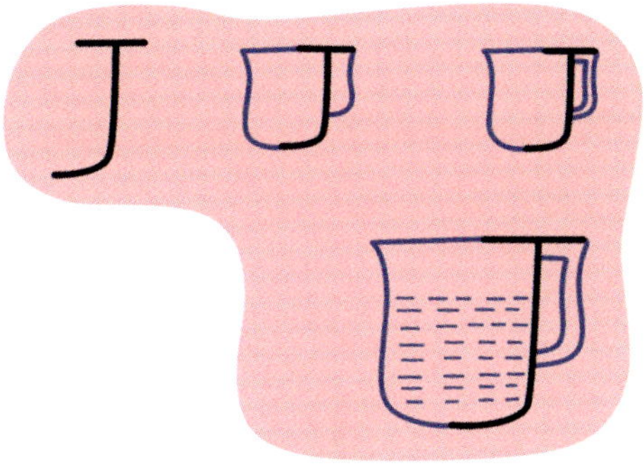

J = Jug

Activity

Let's make a fish with the letter F:

F = Fish

Draw three things using the letter D. Some examples have been given below:

Drawing with Numbers

You have learnt the numbers. Let us draw using numbers 1-9.

5
5
6
6
7
7
8
8
9
9

7. Learn to Draw Scenes

Helping Others Is Always Good

Once upon a time, a bird and a snake lived in a jungle. The snake lived in a hole under the same tree where the bird lived in its nest. The snake was very proud and never spoke to the bird. One day, a big mongoose attacked the snake under the tree. The bird flew at the mongoose and pecked him on the head. The mongoose turned around to see who it was and the snake won the fight. The snake thanked the bird and was always nice and helpful to the bird after that.

Moral of the Story: Even the smallest of us can be useful. So, one should treat everyone nicely and kindly.

How do you draw this story?

This story can be drawn in the following parts:
Draw the bird near its nest in the tree and the snake sitting outside its hole. Draw the mongoose in the grass.

Draw the bird in six easy steps:

Step 1: Draw a circle.

Step 2: Draw a small circle within the big circle to make the eye.

Step 3: Draw the wing as shown.

Step 4: Draw the beak.

Step 5: Draw the second wing.

Step 6: Colour/shade the bird's eye and draw the tail. The bird is ready to fly now.

Draw the snake in six easy steps:

Step 1: Draw a small circle for the head of the snake, and then draw out a guideline for the snake's body as shown below.

Step 2: Now, draw the shape of the snake's head as shown below.

Step 3: Draw an eye, and then make the slits for the nose holes. Then, draw a bold lining for the tongue. Make sure to draw that fork split at the tip.

Step 4: Draw the body of the snake. Begin at the top of the head and draw your way down to the middle section of the body.

Step 5: Finish drawing the body by tapering off to form a tail.

Step 6: There you have finished the drawing of the snake. Colour it as you like it.

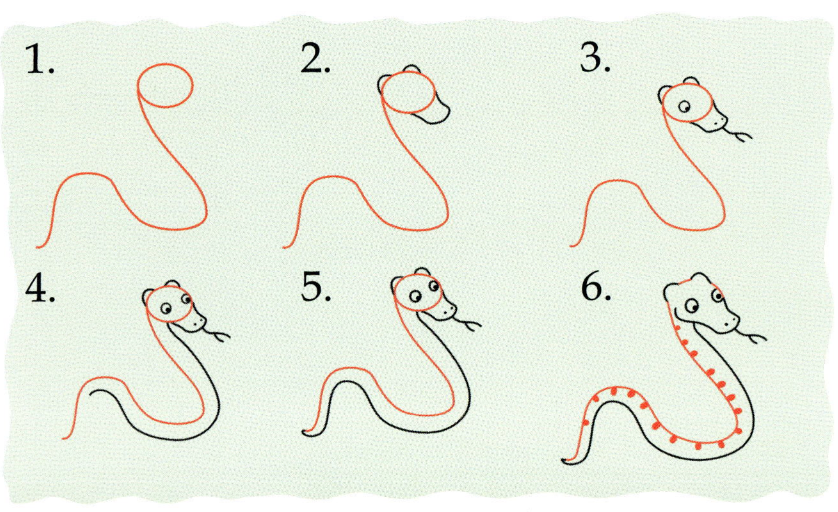

Now, you have learnt to draw the bird and the snake. Follow the illustrations to draw the mongoose in seven steps by yourself.

1.

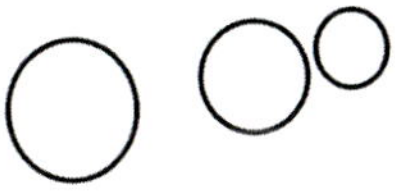

2.

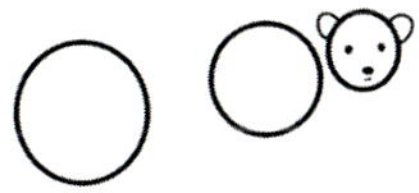

3.

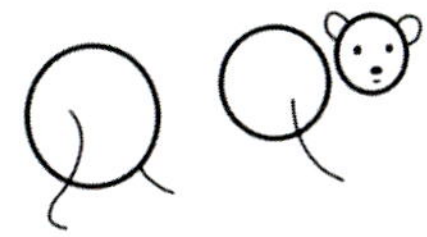

4.

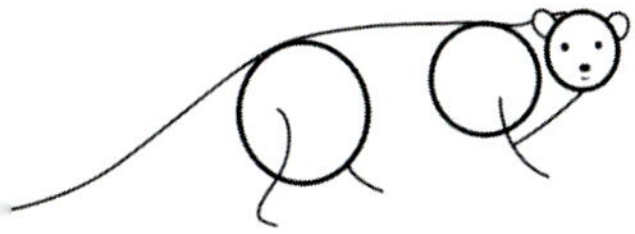

5.

6.

7.

Now, put the story together by drawing the animals and the bird and colouring the final picture. Do not forget to add grass and trees to complete the picture.

Let's Get Active

1. Follow the simple steps and learn to draw a ladybug:

2. Let's draw a penguin with the letter P by using four easy steps. Follow the steps:

Step 1: Make a P.

Step 2: Make the P into a B which will form the belly of the penguin. Draw a circle to form the eye.

Step 3: Shade the eye and draw the penguin's beak. Draw a reverse D behind the B to make the back of the penguin.

Step 4: Colour the penguin to form the black and white body. There! You have P = Penguin.

3. Follow the steps and make a rainy day cloud:

GLOSSARY

Movement	going from one place to another
Create	to make
Activity	to do something